Leadership Success

Turn Your Sales Team Into the Most Productive Team in Your Company. Be a Winner.

Your promotion to leadership level requires a new mindset. All the skills that you have acquired throughout your sales history now have a new application – a new customer – your Sales Team.

In this remarkable Itty Bitty® Book, internationally famous sales performance trainer, Anthony Camacho, shows you how to apply your sales skills to create successful and effective Sales Teams.

You will learn:

- The essentials of coaching your sales team.
- How to motivate your team.
- How to delegate with style.
- How to motivate your team to greater success.

If you want to learn how to apply your sales skills to a higher leadership level, pick up a copy of this revolutionary Itty Bitty® Book today.

Your Amazing
Itty Bitty®
Little Black Book of
Success for Sales Leaders

15 Critical Steps to Greater Results
in Unlocking Your Leadership
Potential

Anthony Camacho
Best Selling Author

Published by Itty Bitty® Publishing
A subsidiary of S & P Productions, Inc.

Printed in the United States of America

Itty Bitty® Publishing
311 Main Street, Suite D
El Segundo, CA 90245
(310) 640-8885

ISBN: 978-0-9987597-4-6

I would like to thank my grandfather, Grandpa Tony Martinez, for teaching me the value of a strong work ethic, my grandmother, Grandma Dora Martinez, for being my first motivational speaker, and my three beautiful princesses – Allasondra, Anastasia and Athena – for completing my purpose.

A very special and heartfelt thank you to my Fairy Godmother, Joan Meijer, for inspiring me to make this a great book. And, a special thank you to Suzy Prudden, my business savvy Fairy Godmother, for pushing me to greater success.

Stop by our Itty Bitty® website to find interesting discussions about Sales Leadership. Find out about Anthony's 12-month VIP Leadership Sales Management Courses.

www.IttyBittyPublishing.com

Or visit Anthony at

http://www.topproducerfactory.com

Be sure to check out Anthony's training videos on YouTube.

Table of Contents

Introduction

It's a great feeling when you earn a promotion and become a Sales Manager. What you can't forget is that the promotion is just the beginning. Starting from the moment you receive that promotion, you must earn the status of leadership with your sales team.

Simply becoming a Sales Manager, CEO, General Manager or Real Estate Broker does not make you a successful sales leader. You are now responsible for the development of the people in your company or on your team. As a Sales Leader you have a great responsibility and obligation to make your sales team and sales organization reach ever-higher levels of success.

You are to be of service to your sales team. Your leadership skills directly affect their mindset and performance. You are to influence their personal and professional growth.

Take all of your selling ability and sell your company objective, goals and yourself to your new *customer* – THE SALES TEAM.

You are not to be a slave to your sales people. You must be of service to them. Your sales leadership directly affects their lifestyle and family time. You, yourself, are a great sales professional or else you would not have been promoted. Just as you got to know the wants and needs of the prospects and customers to get the appointments or to close the deal, you need to do the same thing with you sales team. It's important to have a successful sales team that is not just compliant to you, but are committed to you and the objectives you're selling that directly impact your pay plan.

You and your team are sales professionals who work on commission. The greater the commissions you help your sales team get, the greater commission you make. The reward will include the greater satisfaction of making a positive impact on your sales team's lives. Greatness, results, a culture of winners and solution-based thinking begins with the Sales Leader – YOU.

This is a great and exciting time in your career, because the opportunities are endless.

> *Wishing you all greater success in all areas of your life; personally, professionally and financially.*

Step 1
Your Leadership Vision

As a sales leader, whether you're a CEO, General Manager, Real Estate Broker or entrepreneur – you lead people. If you are a sales leader, this book applies directly to you.

Let's begin with a few questions.

1. What is your personal vision as a leader in your organization?
2. What is it that you want to achieve for yourself?
3. How does your vision affect the way you are perceived by your family?
4. How does your personal vision affect the way you are perceived by your community?
5. How does your personal vision affect the way you are perceived by your business associates and employees?

How does your personal vision affect your own desires? How does it affect your ability to:

- Buy a home?
- Put your kids through college?
- Buy a vacation home?
- Travel the world?
- Be financially independent?

How does your personal vision affect the way you are perceived by your family as a:

- Role model?
- Breadwinner?
- Go-getter?
- Friend?

How does your personal vision affect the way you are perceived by your community, in the areas of:

- Honesty?
- Integrity?
- Dependability?
- Volunteer Work?
- Leadership?

How does your personal vision affect the way you are perceived by your business associates and employees?

- Successful?
- Organized?
- Admirable?
- Problem Solver?
- Great Delegator?
- Skilled Coach?

Step 2
What Is Your Sales Vision?

What is the vision for your winning team? Think bigger than simply managing a process. How do you see them win in, terms of:

1. Constant financial growth.
2. Constantly seeking education.
3. Avoiding complacency.
4. Creating a win-win environment.

What are the goals and measurements you want to develop for your team?

1. Do they have a success plan for each day?
2. Week?
3. Month?
4. Quarter?
5. Year?

What are the success goals and measurements you want for your team?

Daily
- Do they have a success plan for the day?
- Are they maximizing their selling hours?
- Do they know their daily closing ratio?

Weekly
- Are they doing a weekly sales challenge?
- Do they have one-on-one coaching sessions?
- Do they know their weekly closing ratio?
- Do they have beginning week, mid-week and end-of-week progress quotas?

Monthly
- Are they challenging themselves each week of the month to do better than the last week?
- Do they aggressively start selling on the first week instead of starting the third or fourth?
- Do they have monthly incentive contests?

Quarterly
- Do you supply quarterly incentives?
- Do you provide quarterly recognition of your high sales performers?
- Do you have quarterly comparisons to increase sales and additional opportunities?

Yearly
- Do they take a full inventory of products most likely/least likely to sell?
- Which sales personnel grew or failed to grow in performance?
- Do they evaluate what works and what doesn't?

Step 3
How Does Your Sales Team View You?

This view of your attitude and your behavior directly impacts the success, the results and the commission of your sales team.

Are you...?
- Loved?
- Feared?
- Hated?
- Respected?

Do you embody the following positives?

- Do you understand the needs of your team?
- Do you provide supporting sales tools for success?
- Are you a motivator?
- Are you resilient with follow-through?
- Do you maximize the talents and skills of the individuals on your team?

Do you embody these negatives?

- Do you fly off the handle?
- Do you buckle under pressure?
- Do you blame your team for bad sales quotas?
- Are you a bad delegator?
- Are you a bad communicator?

Step 4
Subtract What Is Not Adding Up

Take an honest self-inventory as a sales leader. Identify what areas need improvement and – most importantly – what are you doing that hinders your sales team's performance? Take the time to quietly think about what you can do to improve in these areas. Does your sales team suffer from…?

1. Lack of recognition?
2. Favoritism?
3. Your poor sales incentives?
4. Your poor leadership skills?
5. Your poor sales coaching skills?

Take time to examine what is in your control – things you can personally change to get bigger and better team results.

1. Feeling good about yourself.
2. Feeling good about how you show up in the world.
3. Having a meditative or prayerful life.
4. Seeking additional education about sales.
5. Seeking education about leadership.
6. Seeking education about human behavior.
7. Putting yourself in a position of constant growth.

Take care of yourself:
- Get proper rest.
- Eat healthy food.
- Engage in proper and regular exercise.
- Take vitamins, minerals and healthy supplements.
- Make time for refreshing relaxation, prayer or meditation.
- Make sure that you and your team engage in proactive time management.

Plan ahead for your success. Set goals for:
- Increasing your income.
- What you should do on a daily basis to attain your team's desired unit sales in a week.
- Maximize the hours of a sales team within a day.
- Create efficiencies within the sales team.

Things that you can be aware of for the team:
- When you bring a sales team together, set team objectives at a big team meeting.
- Then schedule a meeting during the week to meet with each sales person to discuss their objectives one-on-one.

Don't blame other people, places or things for failed results.
- As a sales leader, you need to be 100% responsible for your team's results. You can't blame your employer, the customers or the advertising, and you definitely can't blame the sales team.
- Don't contribute to the problem, solve the problem.

Step 5
Your Sales Team is Your Customer

Now you have to manage the Customer Retention Management System (CRM) as it applies to your team. Instead of just simply keeping track of your personal sales numbers, you must keep track of each member's individual sales numbers as well.

CRMs include:
1. Outgoing phone calls
2. Emails
3. Appointments
4. Inventory control
5. Detailed notes about the customer
6. A follow up system

Utilize the CRM system to coach, monitor and mentor each person on the sales team.

Check the CRM throughout the day and throughout the week.

- The salespeople are used to using their CRM to check their individual notes.
- As the sales manager you look at everyone's CRM.
- It becomes your tool to effectively lead each individual on your team.

Use the CRM for strategic follow-up as well.

- The CRM is used to fill the customer data base.
- If your salespeople bring in a new customer, you want to capture that customer's information to build the team's database.

Step 6
Sell the Objective

With your well-deserved promotion, you have gotten a new set of tasks to learn, new processes and procedures to manage. Now you have to be concerned about the sales team's quota, not your personal quota. Don't get lost just being a manager, become a courageous sales leader.

1. You are now a selling machine and your new customer is the sales team itself.
2. Use the sales techniques that you know to sell the company objectives.
3. Think about the selling approaches and techniques that you used with your customers and apply them to your team.
4. Your approaches could include:
    a. Utilizing facts and figures of what works for other teams. How could those facts and figures be used by your team?
    b. Utilizing your personal experiences and successes for reaching sales objectives in the past.
    c. Capitalizing on the credibility of your personal success as applied to the team's sales objectives.

The value of selling your company objectives

Selling the company objectives to your sales team creates an emotional connection to them.

Facts and figures could include:
- Closing ratios
- Market trends
- Consumer buying habits
- What the competition is using for success

Your credibility could include personal experience:
- Sales records broken
- Happy customer success stories
- Proven track record of results
- Your emotional connection
- Recognition of successes among friends and family
- Stories about:
  - Personal gratification and satisfaction
  - Promotions
  - Earning more money
  - Confidence-building techniques

Step 7
Delegate with Style

When delegating to your team, do it with style.

1. Have a very clear and well-defined direction for where you want to lead.
2. Establish what you expect. If you are unsure of what you expect, your sales team will shoot aimlessly in the dark.
3. Be organized and prepared with start times, deadlines, resources, tools and support.
4. Never, ever assume your team can read your mind.
5. Never play favorites.

Everything in selling has a process, including:

- Calling a customer.
- Sending emails.
- Making appointments.
- Taking a credit card application.
- Displaying product.

Delegation has to have a process too:

- Explain
- Demonstrate
- Imitate
- Practice
- Coach
- Correct
- Encourage
- Follow through
- Establish accountability

Step 8
Coaching Your Sales Team

It is vital to coach your sales team one-on-one. Each person on your team has individual needs and obstacles to overcome. Some problems will be more challenging and need more attention than others – this is the nature of the beast.

1. There are many different positions and talents on every team.
2. Each individual needs to be nurtured and developed. No two players on a team are the same.
3. Individual team members may be stronger than others in certain areas, but each team member should be expected to perform every sales activity.
4. Each sales professional is competing with every other sales professional in your team, as well as with every other team in the company.

Essentials of Coaching

- Motivation – The only way you can truly motivate your people is to have a personal relationship with each individual That way you can identify their strengths and build on them.
- Communication – A great number of sales leaders think that they are good at communicating, when what they are good at is talking. Communication includes listening and asking good questions. Communication is a way to genuinely engage – to connect – to identify the strengths, weaknesses, problems, needs of each member. By being a good communicator, you become a great team builder, problem solver and even better listener.
- Encouragement – Through real encouragement – not just a pat on the back – you create a belief in your team that they can have a higher level of success. By setting a challenge for them to reach, and praising them when they reach it, you encourage them to go higher and higher.
- Rewards – Rewards are not just about monetary incentives. Rewards also include peer and upper management recognition.

Make rewards and recognition a big deal.

Step 9
Build Trust with Your Sales Team

Building trust does not mean becoming buddies and hanging out after hours. It means having a genuine concern for your sales team – their ability to achieve greater results, greater success and greater income.

1. Your sales team will do anything for you because they know you'll do anything for them.
2. Stick your neck out for them. When the heat is on, make sure you take the heat.
3. When selling goals are met, make sure they get the praise for hitting their goals from the CEO and co-workers.
4. Be sure not to be a glory-hound. Your sales team's success is your success.

How to Build Trust

Steps for taking the heat:

- When the heat is on, don't throw your team under the bus or into the fire.
- Walk through the fire, with them leading the way.

Your team's success is your success.

- If your team is successful and you give them the credit, they will strive harder and become more successful.
- The people who matter will notice that it is your team that's successful and give you the credit.

Step 10
Accountability is Equal

*"Great Sales Professionals Follow Up
and GREAT Sales Leaders Follow through."*
~ Anthony Camacho

Accountability – *personal* accountability – is
imperative to your team, especially in your role as
their sales leader.

1. Dress for success.
2. Show up on time.
3. Go the extra mile.
4. No extended lunches.
5. Set the example for your team.

If you don't hold your sales people accountable, then
you become an enabler for bad habits and poor
conduct.

1. Accountability – needs to be honored by
   all, including the sales manager.
2. There can be no favoritism or exceptions to
   the rule.

Be very clear about your expectations

- Have a clear start time and have a clear deadline.
- Inspect what you expect.
- Accountability needs to be monitored daily.
- Enforce equally.
  - People should be rewarded for being accountable, and
  - People should be reprimanded for not being accountable.

Step 11
Create a Team of Problem Solvers

There is nothing worse than conducting a counter-productive sales meeting and cry-baby session. There will always be obstacles and hurdles to overcome. Many times your sales team just dumps the fire on your desk and runs off. You have the power to change that dynamic.

Take control of your mindset and give your team a mind shift.

1. Give them the three-to-one rule for problem solving.
2. For every single concern, complaint or obstacle, have them provide you with three solutions.
3. This will create empowerment and independence to think on their own.
4. Challenge your sales team not to report every little problem to upper management. Encourage them to start solving problems by themselves.

Empower your people to think on their own

- Let them make mistakes.
- Encourage positive thinking.
- Have them write down as many solutions as they can for each problem.
- Have them pick their top three solutions.
- Start the problem-solving process with those best three solutions.
- What kinds of problems regularly show up?

Complaints might include:
- Advertising
- Bonuses
- Customers – or the lack thereof
- Lack of product knowledge
- Co-workers
- Work hours
- Inventory or products
- Point of sale material (brochures)
- Communication Skills
- Rotation Systems
- Technology

Teach your team how to use solution-based thinking to handle these complaints or problems.

Step 12
Eliminate Time Robbers

Time robbers are bad habits that rob your sales team from greater selling success and results. Spend time identifying time robbers that affect your team.

1. Time Robbers include:
    a. Personal phone calls
    b. Unproductive social media
    c. Socializing instead of selling
    d. Complaining

2. Another identifier of Time Robbers is:
    a. Which sales tasks are they spending too much time on while not giving the proper attention to the real money makers.

Real Moneymakers Are:

- Getting in front of more customers
- Building a data base
- Making phone calls
- Setting appointments
- Asking for referrals
- Enhancing your closing ratio
- Advertising on social media
- Having your sales tools organized

Step 13
Be Physically Fit to Lead

Having positive and ample amounts of energy stem from being physically fit (which includes being healthy). Fitness gets the best results for yourself and your sales team. If you feel good, you sell great! The same goes for your career as a sales leader; if you feel good, you lead great.

Fitness includes:

1. Having a daily exercise routine
2. Eating healthy
3. Most importantly, getting rest

Health and Fitness Options

Healthy eating:
- Pack a healthy lunch.
- Choose a healthy place to eat.
- Avoid junk food.
- Stay away from sugars – avoid a sugar rush.
- Include daily vitamins, minerals and supplements.
- Avoid hydrogenated oils. Use virgin olive oil.
- Drink plenty of water – 8-10 glasses a day.
- Pack healthy snacks (raw nuts and cheese).
- Eat small amounts throughout the day.
- Eat foods that give you energy.
- Have a high protein diet.
- Stay away from processed food.

Exercise:
- Make time to exercise.
- Walk during lunch.
- Join a local gym.
- Get a personal trainer.

Rest:
- Making time to meditate is a great way to rest. Meditation has three times the rest-benefit of sleep.

Create, encourage and reward these habits with your sales team.

Step 14
Self-Advancement

Continue learning! Learn and master your current position and prepare for the next level up.

1. Develop your mind for greater success and more importantly, for self-satisfaction.
2. This practice creates excitement for your life and you don't become stale in your personal growth and your earning potential.
3. Make it a goal to read personal/professional development books – at least one a month.
4. Listen to audio books, especially if you commute a lot to meet with your customers.
5. Take sales courses, seminars and workshops. You will be surprised at the things you don't know.
6. Include webinars and podcasts in your learning time.
7. Take extension courses at your local college.

Learning

- Schedule certain days during the week for learning.
- Schedule certain times of the day.
- Set the duration of your learning sessions.
- Choose subjects that give you enjoyment.

Which kinds of books and courses are particularly helpful in sales?

Books on:
- Psychology
- Coaching
- Sales
- Leadership
- Communication
- Self-improvement
- Energy
- How to deal with people

It's amazing how many books there are and how many approaches to different subjects there are that can benefit you and add to your sales teams results.

Step 15
Reward Yourself

Take the time to reward yourself for your personal accomplishments and the accomplishments of your sales team. You have the power to make your sales management leadership career rewarding and fulfilling. You have the power to make your work environment fun and full of incentives to reward yourself for a job well done!!!

1. Include the balance of working hard and playing hard in your life and your work.
2. Don't burn yourself out, a situation that becomes counter-productive. This habit affects your family life, sales team and overall happiness.
3. Be present to enjoy your accomplishments.
4. Celebrate your wins. When you stop noticing that you have wins, you become a desensitized machine....

Suggestions for ways to celebrate wins

- Go on a get-away vacation.
- Spend positive time with your family.
- Take yourself out to eat at your favorite restaurant.
- If you like to fish, go fishing.
- Treat yourself and your family to an outing, celebratory dinner or a movie.

Celebrate with your Team.
- Take the team and their families out to a celebratory dinner.
- Suggest team-building exercises outside of work, such as:
    - Obstacle courses
    - Relay races, or even
    - Rowing a boat together

You've finished. Before you go...

Tweet/share that you finished this book.

Please star rate this book.

Reviews are solid gold to writers. Please take a few minutes to give us some itty bitty feedback.

ABOUT THE AUTHOR

Anthony Camacho, also known as the "Hitman," is the CEO/Founder of the Top Producer Factory. In addition he is a motivational speaker, international sales performance coach, leadership sales management trainer, best-selling published author and corporate Emcee. He is a Dale Carnegie Coach and IPEC Certified Professional Coach.

Camacho has completed over 500 on-sight training workshops for multi-million and billion dollar sales organizations. In addition, he provides off-site seminars at Pelican Hill Newport Beach, Wynn Las Vegas, Aria Las Vegas, Hotel Irvine etc. His company has been hired to consult and coach all over the world.

His recently published "Little Black Book of Sales" can be purchased online as a paperback book or as an eBook.

You can also follow him on his new YouTube series, "Sales Tips to Stretch Your Sales Performance." https://youtu.be/8adZQXOpH7E

"You have the power to write your own paycheck in sales."

~Anthony Camacho

At the age of 22, Anthony became the youngest franchise owner for an automotive consulting company. For six consecutive years, he single-handedly generated over $700,000 in total revenue.

The corporate office wanted to continue to utilize Anthony's skills on a much larger scale. At the age of 28, Anthony sold his franchise and later became the youngest Regional Sales Manager in North America.

During his tenure in the corporate office, he was tasked with cold-calling, generating new prospects, bringing in new business, closing deals and managing a sales team.

He consistently achieved the highest new account-closing ratio, which quickly earned him the nickname "The HITMAN."

Anthony attributes his strong work ethic to his grandparents who taught him the value of hard work, perseverance and motivation.

Contact him today for a complimentary sales assessment. Also visit his website www.topproducerfactory.com for more information, including:

- ➤ Sales Performance Coaching
- ➤ Motivational Sales Workshops
- ➤ 90-Day Sales Challenge
- ➤ Top Producer Factory Seminars
- ➤ VIP Leadership Sales Management Training
- ➤ Camacho University Online
- ➤ VIP Leadership Sales Management Courses

If you like this Itty Bitty® book,
you might also enjoy…

- *Best Seller* **Your Amazing Itty Bitty®
  Little Black Book of Sales** – Anthony
  Camacho

- **Your Amazing Itty Bitty® Heal Your
  Body** – Patricia Garza Pinto

- **Your Amazing Itty Bitty® Prospect-to-
  Profit Lead Generation Book** – Erin
  Smilkstein

And other Itty Bitty® Books available online.

www.ingramcontent.com/pod-product-compliance
Lightning Source LLC
Chambersburg PA
CBHW071422200326
41520CB00014B/3535